The Companion Guide to
BEAUTIFUL
GIRLHOOD

32 Character Training Lessons

Shelley Noonan and Kimberly Zach

Pumpkin Seed PRESS

Humphrey, Nebraska 68642

Excerpts taken from the original edition of Mabel Hale's Beautiful Girlhood, Copyright © 1940 by Gospel Publications and the revised edition, Copyright © 1993 by Great Expectations Book Co. Used by permission.

Third printing, 2011

The Companion Guide to Beautiful Girlhood

Copyright © 2000 by Pumpkin Seed Press, LLC
Humphrey. NE 68642

ISBN 0-9700273-0-3

To our daughters

Laura

and

Kelsey

Table of Contents

Introduction

Dear Friends,

Beautiful Girlhood, written by Mabel Hale in the 1940's for girls entering womanhood, has become a classic in home-schooling and Christian circles. A revised version was later adapted by Karen Andreola from the original. This companion guide can be used with either book, although Hale's book contains one more chapter.

Five years ago my daughter Laura and I discovered this book and the value it had for our relationship. Our special time would begin with a cup of tea, as we took turns reading the chapter we would later discuss. It was a way for us to escape the hum of daily life to a time when I could teach with intent the values and principles I found important. It was also an opportunity for her to ask questions and think about the issues that she would soon face as a young girl on the brink of womanhood.

The Companion Guide to Beautiful Girlhood was birthed from this priceless experience. Our vision for this guide has been to create a flexible tool for a mother to use while teaching her daughter important life lessons. The discussion questions are organized so that after you read the chapter together you can talk about the wisdom it contains. The Bible study and activities were designed to

support the topics in the chapter. The Bible study could be done at that time or separately. Finally, the quotations and journaling aspects of this guide are a medium to encourage the daughter to think about what she has just learned and make it her own by articulating her thoughts. This written record of her young womanhood will be a priceless keepsake in later years.

Our prayer is that this will be a special, memorable time for both mother and daughter. There is no right or wrong way to do this study. Let this guide help you find a way that is perfect for your circumstances.

Blessings,

Shelley

February 2000

❧ 1 ❧

A Rose Bud Opens

"Girlhood is the opening flower of womanhood."

Discussion Questions

1. What are the familiar traits of childhood that are charming? What are some funny stories that you or your Mom remember about you as a little girl?

2. Name a few of the "graces and powers of womanhood."

3. Remember that your joyous attitude has a large influence on your family. What are some ways that you demonstrate your joy? Tell of a time when you know your joy was an influence.

4. "Girlhood is a time of making ready. Maturity and independence come later." What are some ways you can use this time to get ready for adulthood? Could the realization that this is a time of preparation make it any easier to patiently wait for maturity and independence?

5. "Dream your bright and happy dreams and aspire to your lofty heights." Mom, what were your dreams when you were your daughter's age? Do you still have dreams? Daughter, what are your dreams?

Bible Activities and Applications

1. Look up these Bible verses and record what they have to say about cheerfulness.

   - Proverbs 15:13
   - Proverbs 15:15
   - Proverbs 15:30

2. Make a list of all the ways you can cheerfully serve each of the members of your family.

3. Ask someone in your family to record every time in one day that you cheerfully serve someone. At the end of the day, count them up with your mom.

Journal Topics

1. Describe an incident when you know your joyous attitude influenced a member of your family. Include details about the result.

2. Choose one of the quotations and explain what you think it means or how it relates to you at this stage of your life.

The rose is fairest when 'tis budding new.
Sir Walter Scott (1771-1832)

Queen rose of the rosebud garden of girls.
Alfred, Lord Tennyson (1809-1832)

Journal Response

❦ 2 ❦

From the Child to the Woman

*"We see this miracle take place continually,
yet we never cease to wonder at the sweetness,
charm, and beauty of every young woman
as she comes to maturity."*

Discussion Questions

1. "The little girl in you has lost interest in her play
   world." What are some "little girl" objects or activities that don't interest you anymore?

2. What are some things that you have wanted to do
   lately that your mother wisely did not give permission for?

3. Besides these emotional changes, your body will soon
   be changing, too. Are you looking forward to these
   changes? (This would be a good time for mom to

explain things if you haven't yet, and also to relate
how you felt at this time in your life.)

4. Explain why "Good women are needed everywhere
and the call for them will never grow faint."

5. Name and describe any "good women" you know or
have read about. What made them "good"?

Bible Activities and Application

1. Read through Proverbs 31. Then go back verse by
verse and list the qualities that make her a role model
for women. (Hint: industrious, frugal, diligent.)

2. Think of someone you know who has some of the
qualities of the Proverbs 31 woman. Write her a note
or a letter telling her of your admiration for her and
why.

Journal Topics

1. What does the phrase "her worth is far above rubies" mean in relation to the lives of the good women you know? What does it mean for your mother and you?

2. Write a paragraph describing one of your happiest childhood experiences. Explain why you think it has remained in your memory so clearly.

3. Explain how you are, or aren't, as the quotation states, "standing with reluctant feet" between childhood and womanhood.

Little girl, my stringbean, my lovely woman.
Anne Sexton (1928-1974)

Standing with reluctant feet, where the
brook and river meet.
Womanhood and childhood fleet.
Henry Wadsworth Longfellow (1807-1882)

Journal Response

❧ 3 ❧

Keeping up Acquaintances

"I want you to see that you are changing and not to expect everyone to change with you."

Discussion Questions

1. In what sense does the author use the word "acquaintance"?

2. Have you ever felt "unacquainted" with your mother?

3. What are some ways in which you can stay acquainted with your mother? With your father? With other members of your family?

4. How is selfishness a hindrance to staying acquainted with people?

5. What are some ways you can fight against selfishness?

Bible Activities and Application

1. Look up these Bible verses and list the behaviors that demonstrate selfishness.

   - 2 Timothy 3:2
   - Romans 15:1
   - 1 Corinthians 10:33
   - Isaiah 56:11
   - 1 John 3:7
   - James 3:14-16

2. Review your list and put a check by the ones that best describe your behavior.

3. Plan an outing or special time with your mother or father that will help you become better acquainted. Write a list of questions that you've always wanted to ask them or things you've always wanted to know about their growing up years.

Journal Topics

1. Write a short essay using the first quote as your first sentence. Use examples from history that demonstrate the truth of the statement.

2. Tell how you see yourself in the second quote.

Selfishness is the greatest curse of the human race.
William Ewart Gladstone (1809-1898)

This is the true joy of life, the being used for a purpose recognized by yourself as a mighty one...instead of a feverish selfish little clod of ailments and grievances complaining that the world will not devote itself to making you happy.
George Bernard Shaw (1856-1950)

Journal Response

❧ 4 ❧

Character-Building

*"The most precious early treasure a girl
can have is good character."*

Discussion Questions

1. Write your own definition of character. Then look up
   the definition of character in a dictionary to see how
   it compares to yours.

2. How is a person's character built? What are some
   experiences that have worked towards the building of
   your character?

3. Discuss the importance of building your character
   now, rather than waiting until you are an adult.

4. List five traits you would like to build into your character.

5. Why is Christ the perfect pattern for character-building?

Bible Activities and Application

1. Look up these Bible verses and write the character traits that each one mentions.

   - Psalm 34:2
   - Psalm 37:26
   - Matthew 5:6
   - Luke 2:25
   - 2 Corinthians 1:12
   - 2 Corinthians 2:17
   - 1 Thessalonians 4:9

2. Choose the trait from your list that you desire most and create a plan to build it into your character this week. Share it with your mother.

Journal Topics

1. Make a chart that shows your positive character traits. Give examples of what you do that exemplifies each trait. Do the same with the traits you wish you had and write examples of what you could do to get them.

2. Explain whether or not you agree with Anne Frank's quote. Make sure to cite several reasons that support your opinion.

It is our duty to compose our character not to compose books, and to win, not battles and provinces, but order and tranquility for our conduct of life.
Montaigne (1553-1592)

Parents can only give good advice or put them (children) on right paths, but the final forming of a person's character lies in their own hands.
Anne Frank (1929-1945)

Journal Response

❧ 5 ☙

The Strength of Obedience

*"The girl who would come to perfect womanhood
must learn to be obedient."*

Discussion Questions

1. "All the universe is under obedience." What makes
   humans' obedience different from the obedience fol-
   lowed by the rest of nature?

2. What are the two kinds of obedience? Recall a time
   when you were obedient in action, but not in your
   heart.

3. Give three reasons why a girl who wants to come to
   perfect womanhood must learn to be obedient.

4. Has learning the lesson of obedience been a hard battle for you or an easy one? Explain.

5. Name the benefits of a mother's obedience and a daughter's obedience. How are they alike and how are they different?

6. Why must it be you who "takes herself in hand and conquers" disobedience? Why can't it be anyone else's responsibility?

Bible Activities and Application

1. Use the Bible verses to answer the questions.

   From where should obedience come?
   - Deuteronomy 11:13
   - Romans 6:17

   What should be the attitude of obedience?
   - Joshua 22:2-3
   - Psalm 119:34
   - Isaiah 1:19
   - Phillipians 2:12

2. Make a list of all the people who are in authority over areas of your life. Write all the ways that you can honor them by being obedient. Then put them into action.

Journal Topics

1. Recall a time in the past when you were not obedient. Review the situation in light of scripture. Make sure to note the consequences.

2. Describe the ways in which you see obedience as a way of adding strength to your character.

He who longs to strengthen his spirit must go beyond obedience and respect.
Constantine Peter Cavafy (1863-1933)

The strongest is never strong enough to be always the master, unless he transforms his strength into right, and obedience into duty.
Jean Jaques Rousseau (1712-1778)

Journal Response

❧ 6 ❧

Making Herself Beautiful

*"A desire to be beautiful is not unwomanly...
but, mark you, true beauty is not of the face,
but of the soul."*

Discussion Questions

1. How would you define godly beauty as opposed to worldly beauty? Which of the two is more to be sought and admired?

2. Can the search for the physical be taken too far? To what extent should you go to care for your physical self?

3. What truly makes hands beautiful? feet? face?

4. Name some women you know who possess beauty of the soul rather than the face.

5. Explain why a pretty face without true beauty of the soul is a dangerous gift.

Bible Activities and Application

1. Use these Bible verses to answer the questions.

   Where is beauty found?
   ☙ Proverbs 31:30
   ☙ 1 Peter 3:3-4

   What does real beauty look like?
   ☙ 1 Peter 3:3-6

   What are some of the things that could be mistaken for beauty?
   ☙ 1 Peter 3:3

2. Read about Sarah's life in Genesis and explain how she personified beauty.

Journal Topics

1. Write about a woman you know whose inner beauty shines outwardly. Tell how it makes her appear physically beautiful.

2. What are some things you can do now to assure that you will concentrate on beautifying your inner self more than your outward self? Write these suggestions down so that you can refer to them when you need to be reminded.

Good nature is more agreeable in conversation than wit, and gives a certain air to the countenance which is more amiable than beauty.
Joseph Addison (1672-1719)

Kindness in women, not their beauteous looks, shall win my love.
William Shakespeare (1564-1616)

Journal Response

❧ 7 ❧

Watch Your Tongue

"A girl is known by her words."

Discussion Questions

1. How is it true that a girl is known by her words? What impressions have your words left with those who know you?

2. How does an uncontrolled tongue result in damage to family and friends?

3. Describe a time when you failed to control your tongue and the damage you caused.

4. In the way that obedience must come from within, so must you control your words. Name two things you can actively do to control your tongue.

5. When does natural curiosity about our neighbors and friends become hurtful gossip?

Bible Activities and Application

1. Look up these passages which show positive ways to use the tongue. Explain why they are positive.

   - Proverbs 12:18b
   - Proverbs 12:25
   - Proverbs 15:1
   - Proverbs 16:23-24

2. Study James 3. List all the things it says about the tongue. Consider what this means for your life.

3. This week be especially aware of the impact your words have on others. Take the time to carefully consider their effect before you speak. Perhaps you can even choose one or two people whom you can uplift with the spoken word. Then do it.

Journal Topics

1. Write a commentary on the phrase "tonguelashing." What images does it bring to mind?

2. List some situations which show the power words carry. Some examples to get you started are a mother soothing a baby, song lyrics, and greeting cards. Recall specific examples of these and describe them as positive or negative.

A sharp tongue is the only edge tool that grows keener with constant use.
Washington Irving (1783-1859)

It hurteth not the tongue to give fair words.
John Heywood (1497-1580)

Journal Response

_____

_____

_____

_____

_____

_____

_____

_____

_____

_____

_____

_____

_____

_____

_____

_____

_____

_____

_____

_____

_____

_____

_____

_____

_____

_____

_____

_____

_____

_____

_____

❧ 8 ❧

A Sunny Disposition

*"The world has enough tears and
sorrow at best, and a girl's sweet,
smiling face can scatter untold clouds."*

Discussion Questions

1. What is meant by the phrase "sunshine maker"?
   What are you able to do if you have mastered the art
   of being sunny?

2. Which events in life are true tests of a sunny disposi-
   tion…the deep shadows or the little irritations?
   Explain.

3. What influence can a tear-chasing smile have?

4. How does one look on the bright side no matter
   what?

5. Why can the faces of other people be called mirrors of our own faces?

Bible Activities and Application

1. Look up the following verses and list the benefits of a joyful heart.

   - Proverbs 14:30
   - Proverbs 15:13
   - Proverbs 15:15
   - Proverbs 15:30
   - Proverbs 17:22

2. Read Philippians 2:14-15. Paraphrase the verses in writing, personalizing a message to yourself about how you are to serve and why.

Journal Topics

1. How does a sunny outlook affect a household? Name five specific things you can do to "live in the sunshine" in your home.

2. Look again at the quote by Stevenson. Write your ideas concerning the meaning of his words.

Look for the silver lining
Whene'er a cloud appears in the blue
Remember somewhere the sun is shining
And so the right thing to do is make it shine
for you.
P.G. Wodehouse (1881-1975)

There is no duty we so much underrate as the
duty of being happy.
Robert Louis Stevenson (1850-1894)

Journal Response

_____
_____
_____
_____
_____
_____
_____
_____
_____
_____
_____
_____
_____
_____
_____
_____
_____
_____
_____
_____
_____
_____
_____
_____
_____
_____
_____
_____

❧ 9 ❧

The Beauty of Truthfulness

"Truth is the foundation of all things…when truth is gone, all that can be relied upon is gone."

Discussion Questions

1. Why is a life "worse than useless" if it lacks the element of truth?

2. In what ways does truth beautify?

3. What are the root causes of a lie?

4. What is the most common lie? the meanest kind of lie? the silliest kind of lie? Give examples of each kind of lie.

5. How does a girl who does not always speak the truth put herself in a position to be continually mistrusted? How does this apply at home, school, and work?

Bible Activities and Application

1. Look up these Bible verses and list the benefits of truthfulness.

   ❧ Proverbs 12:17,19,22

   ❧ Proverbs 14:5, 7, 25

   ❧ 1 Peter 2:12

2. Recall and/or re-read the lives of Abraham, Isaac, and Jacob. Note the pattern of dishonesty in each of their lives and how it affected those they loved. Record the Bible reference for each.

Journal Topics

1. Interview a parent or grandparent about an experience they have had with honesty or dishonesty. Write about the results.

2. Think about the following questions and relate them to your life: Why does the saying "always speak the truth" not necessarily mean "all the truth should always be spoken"? In what situations would speaking the truth be offensive? Why are some truths better left unsaid?

He who permits himself to tell a lie once, finds it much easier to do it a second and third time, till at length it becomes habitual...this falsehood of the tongue leads to that of the heart.
Thomas Jefferson (1743-1826)

The heart should have fed upon the truth, as insects on a leaf...
Samuel Taylor Coleridge (1772-1834)

Journal Response

_____
_____
_____
_____
_____
_____
_____
_____
_____
_____
_____
_____
_____
_____
_____
_____
_____
_____
_____
_____
_____
_____
_____
_____
_____
_____
_____
_____

❦ 10 ❦

Sincerity

*"To be sincere is to be in reality
what one appears to be: not feigned;
not assumed; genuine, real, and true."*

Discussion Questions

1. What does it mean to be sincere?

2. In what ways might a person be dishonest with herself?

3. Explain why being truly honest is not always the "easiest path."

4. How are a handshake, smile, and eye contact measures of sincerity? What are some physical signs of insincerity?

5. Name some examples of ways a person can be insincere in her work.

Bible Activities and Application

1. Write the consequences or benefits that these verses reveal about the seriousness of dishonesty.

   - Proverbs 6:16-17

   - Proverbs 11:9

   - Proverbs 12:22

   - 1 Thessalonians 4:12

   - Revelation 21:8

2. Look up these verses and write down God's standards for honesty.

   - Proverbs 19:5

   - Proverbs 21:6

   - Ecclesiastes 5:4-6

   - 2 Corinthians 8:21

3. Read Proverbs 26:28. Think about how a lying tongue shows hatred to those who are its victims. Recall any examples you have observed.

Journal Topics

1. Write about a time when you were caught in an act of dishonesty. Describe the consequences and the lesson you learned from it.

2. Choose one of the quotations and write a short commentary on what you think it means.

How happy is he born and taught,
That serveth not another's will
Whose armor is his honest thought,
And simple truth his utmost skill.
Sir Henry Wotton (1568-1639)

Many a man's reputation would not know his
character if they met on the street.
Elbert Hubbard (1856-1915)

Journal Response

॰ 11 ॰

Ideals

"So it is imperative that a girl set before her good and pure ideals, that she set her mark high. It is better to aim at the impossible than to be content with the inferior."

Dicussion Questions

1. Explain how ideals will shape a woman's life. Describe what might happen when ideals are aimed too low.

2. What is the Christian pattern for the ideal woman? List the elements of the pattern.

3. "The best cannot be gained without effort." What are some of the areas you would like to develop in order to fulfill your ideals?

4. What does it mean to pursue something wholeheartedly? Recall a time when you pursued an interest in this way. How can you use that experience to model your efforts now?

5. Having ideals is the first step but what must follow?

Bible Activities and Application

1. Consider what God's word has to say about looking ahead to the goals for your life.

   - Psalm 27:4
   - Philippians 3:13-14
   - Colossians 3:1-2
   - Hebrews 12:1-2

2. Why is it easy to "become blinded by the glitter and gloss of things that are not pure gold"? What books, TV shows, magazines, music, and movies do you pay attention to? Do these things affect your image of the ideal woman?

Journal Topics

1. Write a reaction to the verses you looked at in the Bible Activities and Application. Include what your goals are and how they connect with the ultimate goal of serving and doing God's word.

2. Write a description of the life you would live as a biblical "ideal woman."

The Christian ideal, it is said, has not been tried and found wanting; it has been found difficult and left untried.
G.K. Chesterton (1874-1936)

Ideals are like stars, you will not succeed in touching them with your hands. But like the seafaring man on the desert of waters, you choose them as your guides, and following them, you will reach your destiny.
Carl Schurz (1829-1906)

Journal Response

_____
_____
_____
_____
_____
_____
_____
_____
_____
_____
_____
_____
_____
_____
_____
_____
_____
_____
_____
_____
_____
_____
_____
_____
_____
_____
_____
_____
_____
_____
_____
_____
_____

❧ 12 ❧

Ambition

"But the highest ambition asks that your life be given for the good of mankind."

Discussion Questions

1. Why is ambition the sister of ideals? Explain the differences between ideal and ambition.

2. Name two types of ambition and the motives behind each. Tell which one you want to have and why.

3. No matter what our ambitions, what should the underlying intent always be?

4. What is your ambition? What do you see yourself accomplishing with this ambition?

5. Judge your ambition. Ask yourself, "Is it good, is it noble, is it pure, what is my underlying intent?"

Bible Activities and Application

1. There are more instances in the Bible where ambition is warned against than encouraged. Read the following verses and write down who the verse is talking about, what their sin of ambition was, and what was the consequence.

   ❧ Genesis 3:5-7

   ❧ Numbers 12:1-16

   ❧ Isaiah 14:12-15

2. Jesus gave the pattern for positive ambition. Read about it in Matthew 20:25-26 and Matthew 23:11-12.

3. Look up the word paradox. What are the paradoxes found in the above verses?

4. Read Romans 15:20 and 1 Thessalonians 4:11-12. Explain how they are examples of positive ambition.

Journal Topics

1. Consider whether your ambitions follow the positive pattern encouraged in the Bible. Write what they can mean for your future.

2. Place a copy of these ambitions in a sealed envelope and put it away in a safe place. Plan to open the envelope in ten years as you would a time capsule.

All ambitions are lawful except those which climb upward on the miseries or credulities of mankind.

Joseph Conrad (1857-1924)

*Climb high
Climb far
Your goal the sky
Your aim the star.*

Anonymous

Journal Response

13

The Power of Purpose

"A purpose in life gives one something to live for, something to work for, and something to hope for."

Discussion Questions

1. The three things that make a girl's life a success are ideals, ambition, and purpose. Explain the connection between the three.

2. "A purpose in life gives one something to live for…" How do circumstances affect a life without purpose? Ask your mother what she sees as her purpose in life.

3. What does it mean to have a "worthy purpose"? How can one make her purpose worthy?

4. Why is success dependent on purpose?

5. Ask yourself this important question: What am I living for and what is my purpose?

Bible Activities and Application

1. One way to live with purpose is to set goals. Read Colossians 3:2 and Luke 12:18-19. Compare the two different kinds of goals portrayed in these verses.

2. True success can be defined as doing and knowing God's specific will for your life. According to Ephesians 2:10, what is your purpose?

Journal Topics

1. List five goals that will help you fulfill your purpose in life. Evaluate them according to the verses mentioned in question # 1 on page 59.

2. Read the quote by James Dickey. Describe what it would be like to shake with purpose.

Lord, let me shake with purpose.
James Dickey (1923-1997)

But what if I fail of my purpose here?
It is but to keep the nerves at strain,
To dry one's eye and laugh at a fall,
And, baffled, get up and begin again.
Robert Browning (1812-1889)

Journal Response

_____
_____
_____
_____
_____
_____
_____
_____
_____
_____
_____
_____
_____
_____
_____
_____
_____
_____
_____
_____
_____
_____
_____
_____
_____
_____
_____
_____
_____
_____
_____
_____
_____

❧ 14 ❧

Dreams

"Why do girls dream? Because all life is before them, and they cannot help but anticipate the future that awaits them."

Discussion Questions

1. Describe the role dreams play in character building.

2. What do many dreams of love and romance lack?

3. Think about the dreams you have for your future. What do they say about the priorities in your life?

4. Why do girls dream? What is positive about correct dreaming?

5. What caution does the author give about time spent dreaming? Do you think this caution is wise?

Bible Activities and Application

1. Read Genesis 37; 39-47. As you read, make a list of ways you see Joseph taking action to make his dreams come true.

2. List some ways that you can harness your dreams as Joseph did to make your dreams work for you.

Journal Topics

1. Reflect on these words from the author: "A girl should look ahead to what she expects out of life and endeavor to fit herself to fill the place as it should be filled." Write what those words mean for you and your dreams.

2. What do you think Thoreau meant when he said, "Dreams are the touchstones of our character." Can you relate the dreams you have with your character or the character you wish to have?

If one advances confidently in the direction of his dreams, and endeavors to live the life which he has imagined, he will meet with a success unexpected in common hours.
Henry David Thoreau (1817-1862)

Yet in my dreams I'd be
Nearer, my God, to Thee
Nearer to Thee.
Sarah Flower Adams (1805-1848)

Journal Response

❧ 15 ❧

Friendships

"A person is made better or worse by his friends."

Discussion Questions

1. Explain the comparison between the growth of friendship and that of a plant.

2. Why is an old friend more to be prized than a new one?

3. Explain each statement that follows and relate one or two incidents from your life that show their truth.

   ❧ A person is made better or worse by his friends.

❧ A girl should have many friends but only a very few intimate friends.

4. What does a mother have to offer as a confidante that a friend may not have?

5. What are the dangers in becoming too familiar with boys as friends?

Bible Activities and Application

1. Look up the following verses and list the characteristics of a godly friendship.

   ❧ 1 Samuel 18:1

   ❧ Proverbs 14:7

   ❧ Proverbs 27:6, 9, 17

   ❧ Ecclesiastes 7:3-4

   ❧ Amos 3:3

   ❧ 2 Corinthians 6:14

   ❧ 1 Thessalonians 5:15

   ❧ 2 Thessalonians 3:6

   ❧ 1 Peter 5:5

2. Think of your oldest friend and describe the reasons you prize her friendship.

Journal Topics

1. Reflect on a close friendship you now enjoy or had in the past. Describe how it first took root, then flourished and grew.

2. Choose one of the quotes for this chapter or this additional quote by Samuel Johnson (1709 -1784): "A man, Sir, should keep his friendship in constant repair." Write how one of these sayings is applicable to the experiences you have had with friendships.

A friend may well be reckoned the masterpiece of Nature.
Ralph Waldo Emerson (1803-1882)

An open foe may prove a curse But a pretended friend is worse.
John Gay (1685-1732)

We read that we ought to forgive our enemies, but we do not read that we ought to forgive friends.
Cosimo De Medici (1389-1464)

Journal Response

❧ 16 ❧

An Accomplished Girl

"The most useful accomplishments are within the reach of every energetic, enterprising girl."

Discussion Questions

1. Listed below are accomplishments the author calls useful. Explain the individual advantages of having each one.

   - ❧ keeping house
   - ❧ cooking meals
   - ❧ laundry
   - ❧ sewing

2. How will doing these tasks give a girl a more appreciative attitude towards her mother and others who perform these honorable services for a living?

3. Why is it also important for a girl to learn a way of earning wages?

4. What are the business aspects of running a household? Why should a girl be practiced in these types of skills as well?

5. What are the aspects of entertaining in your home and being a hostess?

Bible Activities and Application

1. Read Proverbs 31:10-31 and list the woman's useful accomplishments.

2. Make a list of the useful accomplishments you have mastered. Then write a list of the ones you need to master yet.

3. Look at your list of unmastered skills. Choose one area (housekeeping, household business, or entertaining) and design a project to help you become accomplished in this area. Example: create a monthly budget for groceries and implement it or balance a checkbook.

Journal Topics

1. Write a short essay about the Proverbs 31 woman. Do you think she could really exist? Is she a literal or figurative person?

2. What kind of wage-earning jobs have you performed? Write about the accomplishments inherent in each of these jobs.

Let us, then, be up and doing,
With a heart for any fate;
Still achieving, still pursuing,
Learn to labor and to wait.
Henry Wadsworth Longfellow (1807-1882)

Knowledge may give weight, but acomplishments give luster, and many more people see than weigh.
Earl of Chesterfield (1694-1773)

Journal Response

❧ 17 ❧

The Oils of Life

*"If there is not in our lives the oils that
lubricate the machinery of life, we shall be
unable to make progress."*

Discussion Questions

1. List five oils of life and explain how they make life operate more smoothly.

2. Examine the list just made and give two concrete examples from your life of how to act out each oil.

3. How do you know when your oil cup is getting low?

4. Where are fresh supplies of these oils available?

5. Describe a situation in which the oils of life were missing. In contrast, describe a time when the oils were used to ease friction.

Bible Activities and Application

1. Look up the following verses and answer these questions about the oil of kindness.

   - Proverbs 11:17
     Who does a kind person benefit?

   - Proverbs 12:25
     How do kind words affect people?

   - Proverbs 14:21, 31
     What happens when you are kind to others in need?

2. What do the following verses tell you about the heart attitude behind politeness?

   - Romans 12:10
   - Galatians 5:13
   - Ephesians 5:21
   - Philippians 2:3-4
   - 1 Peter 5:5

3. Think of a person who is nice to be with. Observe their manners and how they treat others. Evaluate your manners in light of theirs.

Journal Topics

1. Check out a book of basic manners, like *Polite Moments* by Gary Maldaner or *The Little Book of Christian Character and Manners* by William and Colleen Dedrick. Write down the manners you would like to develop.

2. Do you think people today find it unnecessary to have nice manners? How does this affect day to day living, like waiting in line or driving on a busy street? Comment on this.

Life is short, but there is always time for courtesy.

Ralph Waldo Emerson (1803-1882)

The happiness of life is made up of minute fractions—the little soon forgotten charities of a kiss or smile, a kind look, a heartfelt compliment, and the countless infinitesimals of pleasurable and genial feeling.

Samuel Taylor Coleridge (1772-1834)

Journal Response

_____

_____

_____

_____

_____

_____

_____

_____

_____

_____

_____

_____

_____

_____

_____

_____

_____

_____

_____

_____

_____

_____

_____

_____

_____

_____

_____

_____

_____

❧ 18 ☙

Home Life

*"Home is a kind of kingdom with rulers, laws,
and subjects, each with a part to perform
in order that life there shall be perfect,
or at least the best it can be."*

Discussion Questions

1. What images come to your mind when you hear the word house? When you hear the word home? Do these images differ?

2. In the patriarchal governing of a home, while parents have the authority, they must also bear responsibility. Explain why these two go hand in hand.

3. Why will a girl of your age find it a struggle to comply with her parents' decisions?

4. What is the correct way to submit to parental authority?

5. What are some ways you can stay in acquaintance with your father and develop a closer relationship?

6. Until what point should a girl welcome her mother's advice? Why?

Bible Activities and Application

1. Read Ephesians 6:1-3 and answer the following questions.

   ~♥ What does this command you to do?

   ~♥ How does it say it should be done?

   ~♥ What are the benefits of doing things the way God commands?

   ~♥ Who do the authorities in your life represent?

2. Read Psalm 40:6-8. What does it say about how you are to obey?

Journal Topics

1. Evaluate and write about your obedience to your parents in the days that follow this lesson in light of the verses you studied on page 79.

2. Write about the ways in which a girl can influence her siblings in the home for good or bad.

The sober comfort, all the peace which springs from the larger aggregate of little things, on these small cares of daughter, wife, or friend, the almost sacred joys of home depend.
Hannah More (1745-1833)

Mid pleasures and palaces though we may roam, be it ever so humble, there's no place like home.
J.H. Payne (1791-1852)

Journal Response

_____
_____
_____
_____
_____
_____
_____
_____
_____
_____
_____
_____
_____
_____
_____
_____
_____
_____
_____
_____
_____
_____
_____
_____
_____
_____
_____
_____
_____
_____
_____
_____

❧ 19 ❧

A Conversation on Dress

*"One of the first evidences of a real lady is
that she should be modest."*

Discussion Questions

1. What guidelines does the author offer for modest
   dress?

2. Ask your mother to discuss what her position on
   clothing is and set some guidelines for you. Take a
   mental look at your wardrobe and ask each other the
   following questions.

   ❧ Are my clothes modest?

   ❧ Do they reveal too much?

   ❧ Do I like to startle or cause a stir?

- Would a modest woman wear this?

- Could I give boys/men the wrong idea with this item of clothing?

- Am I doing my duty in allowing/wearing this particular garment?

- Am I safe from base comments in wearing this?

3. Make list of reasons that support dressing modestly.

Bible Activities and Application

1. Modesty is an expression of our inner attitude. Read Proverbs 7 and list the characteristics displayed by this woman.

2. The woman in Proverbs 7 is dressed like a harlot. What do you think she is wearing?

3. Memorize 1 Peter 3:3-6.

4. How should we adorn ourselves?

- 1 Timothy 2:9-10
- 1 Timothy 5: 10

Journal Topics

1. Explain whether or not you are like the person described in the first quote below.

2. Write how the second quote reveals the beauty of God's creation and how nothing man can create will ever compare.

Those who make their dress a principal part of themselves, will, in general, become of no more value than their dress.
William Hazlitt (1778-1830)

Let me dress'd fine as I will
Flies, worms, and flowers
Exceed me still.
Isaac Watts (1674-1748)

Journal Response

_____
_____
_____
_____
_____
_____
_____
_____
_____
_____
_____
_____
_____
_____
_____
_____
_____
_____
_____
_____
_____
_____
_____
_____
_____
_____
_____
_____
_____
_____
_____

❧ 20 ❧

When a Girl Goes Out

"…a girl does well to see that everything that concerns her dress and behavior when away from her home…is decent, clean, modest, and quiet."

Discussion Questions

1. Why must a girl consider this statement before she appears in public: "A girl is generally taken at face value."

2. Girls today are allowed much more freedom in going out compared to their mothers and grandmothers. Why is this a two-sided coin?

3. Discuss the author's suggestions for proper physical appearance.

4. What are the author's suggestions for proper behavior?

5. What are the dangers behind flirtation?

Bible Activities and Application

1. Purity is expressed in many different ways, as is modesty. Look again at the women portrayed in Proverbs 7 and Proverbs 31.

2. Make a chart to allow you to see clearly the differences between these two women. Use these elements to compare and contrast them:

   ❧ dress

   ❧ speech

   ❧ goals

   ❧ attitude

   ❧ effect on others

   ❧ behavior towards family

   ❧ attitude towards God.

3. List the benefits of a pure and virtuous life.

Journal Topics

1. Describe a person you know who has a pure heart.

2. Make a list of items or things in nature that are considered pure. Are they more valuable because they are pure? Explain what happens when their purity is obliterated or lost.

My strength is as the strength of ten,
Because my heart is pure.
Alfred, Lord Tennyson (1809-1892)

Purity of soul cannot be lost without consent.
St. Augustine (350-430 A.D.)

Journal Response

_____
_____
_____
_____
_____
_____
_____
_____
_____
_____
_____
_____
_____
_____
_____
_____
_____
_____
_____
_____
_____
_____
_____
_____
_____
_____
_____
_____
_____
_____
_____

♍ 21 ♌

A New Awakening

"When a girl reaches the age of being accountable to God, she has begun to feel the need of higher help in order always to have strength to do right."

Discussion Questions

1. Explain what "the new awakening" is.

2. Has the new awakening happened to you yet? If so, describe how and when this occurred. Ask your mother to share her new awakening experience.

3. Discuss in detail and give examples why a girl may find herself unable to do what she should do. What is the remedy for this dilemma?

4. As a girl begins to see her duty before God, what also becomes more clear?

5. Define "conviction." What happens if it is yielded to? What is the result if it is not yielded to?

6. What follows an act of repentance?

Bible Activities and Application

1. Read each verse and answer the questions.

   Are you good enough to enter heaven?
   ❧ Romans 3:23

   How did God demonstrate his love? Who did Christ die for?
   ❧ Romans 5:8

   What is the cost of sin? What is the gift God offered through the death of His son?
   ❧ Romans 6:23

   What must you do to be saved?
   ❧ Romans 10:9-10

   How are you saved? By works?
   ❧ Ephesians 2:8-9

2. Have you personally received Christ as your savior? Today you have the opportunity to become Christ's child. Pray now to confess your sin and your need for Jesus.

Journal Topics

1. Write down the prayer you prayed today or a reaffirmation of the prayer you prayed when you first accepted the Lord.

Awake my soul! Stretch every nerve
And press with vigor on;
A heavenly race demands thy zeal,
And an immortal crown.
Philip Doddridge (1702-1751)

Sing my tongue, the Savior's glory,
Of his Flesh the mystery sing,
Of the Blood, all price exceeding,
Shed by our immortal king.
Thomas Aquinas (1125-1274)

Journal Response

❦ 22 ❦

A Christian Life

"The life of a Christian is not too hard for a girl to live, if she has the right start and God's help."

Discussion Questions

1. List the character traits of a Christian girl.

2. How have you taken Christ as your example and guide? Can you and your mother list some scenarios that you have experienced?

3. Do you have a time set aside for devotions? Give some reasons why this time is most helpful.

4. What is a way that a girl can commune with God? Is prayer easy or difficult for you? Why?

5. Why do some people behave morally even though they are not professing Christians?

Bible Activities and Application

1. Read Proverbs 2:4-5. How are we told to seek God's word? What will happen if we do this?

2. Read Job 23:12. God's word is more important than what?

3. Read Psalm 119:11 and Joshua 1:8. What are the benefits of memorizing God's word? Where are we to do this?

Journal Topics

1. Start your own notebook to record your quiet times. Here are four things to write down when studying God's word:

   - ❧ **Remember** God's instructions (Proverbs 4:13)

   - ❧ **Do** what God commands (John 14:23-24)

   - ❧ **Tell** others of God's wondrous works, which you have recorded (Psalm 78:4)

   - ❧ **Question** and **Record** what you want to understand; ask someone who might know (Ecclesiastes 7:25 and James 1:5)

The love of wealth makes bitter men;
the love of God, better men.
W.L. Hudson (1849-1919)

Live while you live the epicure would say
And seize the pleasures of the present day;
Live while you live the sacred preacher cries,
And give to God each moment as it flies.
Lord, in my view let both united be,
I live in pleasure when I live in thee.
Thomas Aquinas (1701-1751)

Journal Response

_____
_____
_____
_____
_____
_____
_____
_____
_____
_____
_____
_____
_____
_____
_____
_____
_____
_____
_____
_____
_____
_____
_____
_____
_____
_____
_____
_____
_____
_____
_____

23

The Quiet Hour

*"For all these wearinesses,
the quiet hour is a blessed balm."*

Discussion Questions

1. What value does the quiet hour have for a girl's body? for her mind? for her spirit?

2. What are some methods of experiencing quiet time physically? intellectually? spiritually?

3. Why should quiet time be a regular part of each day, not just when you are feeling frazzled?

4. How do prayer and meditation go hand in hand?

5. Why is it essential to learn to be comfortable being alone?

Bible Activities and Application

1. Read the following verses and write what you believe God is teaching you about prayer.

   ⇄ Psalm 27:11; 50:14-15; 102:1; 117:1

   ⇄ Matthew 5:44; 7:11; 26:41

   ⇄ Luke 10:2; 11:2b-4a

   ⇄ Romans 10:1

   ⇄ Philippians 4:6

2. Begin your own quiet time with conversations with God. Write down prayer requests and answers to prayer.

3. Compile a list of meditation verses. You might begin by looking up "meditation" in your concordance.

Journal Topics

1. Reflect on one or two of the verses on page 99. Write your thoughts.

2. Write a list of all the activities you engage in during a typical week. Is there anything preventing you from having the quiet time you need? Is there something you can eliminate from your schedule?

O that I had wings like a dove; for then would I flee away, and be at rest.
Prayer Book (1662)

I love tranquil solitude,
And such society
As is quiet, wise, and good
Percy Bysse Shelley (1792-1822)

Journal Response

❧ 24 ☙

Making Friends of Books

"…the books she reads will give to one a true estimate of that girl's character."

Discussion Questions

1. What can books provide in the way of becoming acquainted with people who have had a positive influence on the world?

2. How are the books a girl reads a reflection on her?

3. Why should a girl be prudent in her choice of books?

4. What kinds of questions can be asked to test whether a book is the kind of book a girl should read?

5. List five types of books and the benefits or detriments of each.

Bible Activities and Application

1. Read Philippians 4:8. Explain the ways in which this verse can be applied to the books you read.

2. Practice meditating on this verse during your quiet time.

3. See if you can find a book list for recommended reading for girls your age. Have you read any of them?

4. Start to create your own list of books you have read. Make a separate list of books you wish to read. Evaluate your booklist according to the verse in #1 above.

5. As your booklist grows, consider using 3x5 cards and a file box to organize what you have read. In addition to title and author, you can write a brief summary and commentary about each book.

Journal Topics

1. Write about a favorite book and describe how it passes the test for what a girl ought to read.

2. Choose one of the quotes and explain what you think it means or how true it is.

A book is the best of friends, the same today and forever.

Martin Tupper (1810-1889)

Life being very short; and the quiet hours of it few, we ought to waste none of them in reading valueless books.

John Ruskin (1819-1900)

Journal Response

❧ 25 ❧

Waking of the Love-Nature

"This new nature that is waking should be thought of as a beautiful plant given of God to be protected and cherished till it has become large and strong."

Discussion Questions

1. Share with your mother your first memory of her. Mother, share the story of your daughter's birth or adoption.

2. What causes the awakening of the love nature?

3. What is the difference in behavior between boys and girls at this age?

4. Even though the love nature has a girl yearning to experience love, why is it wisest to wait until she is older?

5. Explain the plant analogy used by the author.

6. What are the advantages to submitting to your parents' guidance in this area?

Bible Activities and Application

1. Read Genesis 24. Note how Isaac and Rebecca's relationship began. Who was in control? What was Isaac's attitude? Rebecca's? What role did his parents play? What role did her parents play?

2. Read Judges 14. Note how Samson went about his quest for a Philistine wife. What was Samson's attitude? What role did his parents play in his finding a wife?

3. Both of these situations are examples of how God brought men and women together. Which of these ways would you prefer and why?

4. Compare how the above methods are similar and different from today's customs.

Journal Topics

1. Write about your recognition of the waking of the love nature in yourself and your friends.

2. Write a note to your parents thanking them for the position they have taken in regards to dating.

Who loves a garden still his Eden keeps,
Perennial pleasures plants and wholesome
harvest reaps.
Amos Bronson Alcott (1799-1888)

Daughters of Jersualem... Do not arouse or
awaken love until it desires.
King Solomon, Song of Songs 2:7

Journal Response

❧ 26 ☙

Boy Friends

"All through her early teens the girl is better off with many friends, both of boys and girls."

Discussion Questions

1. How does a girl's attitude towards boys change as she becomes a teen?

2. Describe the boundaries between friendships of boys and girls at this age.

3. What are the advantages of having "frank friendships" with boys?

4. Why is it important for mixed groups to have adults present at their gatherings? How do you feel about being chaperoned?

5. How does a girl's character influence the boys around her?

Bible Activities and Application

1. Read 1 Timothy 5:1-2. How should a girl treat boys who are her friends?

2. Evaluate your friendships with boys under this standard. List the ways the friendships could be improved.

Journal Topics

1. Describe a current friendship that you have with a boy.

2. Think about the friendships you have with girls and then compare and contrast them with the friendships you have experienced with boys. How are they alike and how are they different?

It is the things in common that make relationships enjoyable, but it is the little differences that make them interesting.
Todd Ruthman (unknown)

What is a friend? A single soul dwelling in two bodies.
Aristotle (394-322 BC)

Journal Response

❧ 27 ❧

The Girl Who Can Be Trusted

"What a strength of character she has for her young life's beginning if she has learned to keep her word exactly, to be trustworthy."

Discussion Questions

1. Define what it means to be trustworthy.

2. What often happens when a person lies? Have you ever heard the saying, "Oh, what a tangled web we weave when first we practice to deceive"?

3. What are the advantages to a girl's reputation when she goes where she tells her parents she is going?

4. What did Laura's father say he must do if, after one more chance, she had not learned to master herself?

5. What do you think were Laura's "new insights into trustworthiness"? What does it mean to "purpose in your heart" the decision to be trustworthy?

Bible Activities and Application

1. Read Proverbs 6:16-19 What are the seven things the Lord hates? How many have to do with lying?

2. Read Proverbs 12:22. What does God say about lying? How does God feel about those who act truthfully?

3. How do these verses advise you to handle lying?

   - Psalm 30:8
   - Psalm 101:7
   - Psalm 119:29
   - Proverbs 13:5

Journal Topics

1. Outline the steps you have taken to ensure that you are becoming a girl who can be trusted.

2. Look at the second quote and think about it carefully. Explain the degree of truth it contains.

The essence of lying is deception, not words.
John Ruskin (1819-1900)

The easiest person to deceive is oneself.
Edward Bulwer-Lytton (1803-1873)

Journal Response

❧ 28 ❧

Getting Ready for the Great Responsibility

"Likewise, the calling to be a wife and mother is high, and deserves much preparation."

Discussion Questions

1. Why does it seem that a desire for children is inbred in all women?

2. In what ways does a wife complement her husband?

3. Explain this about motherhood: "It is a life-long job and one that will tell for good or bad to the end of time."

4. Aside from physical preparation, what are the things a girl can do to mentally prepare for motherhood and wifehood?

5. List five things you are doing now to help prepare for the great responsibility. Then think of five more things you can begin doing and add them to your list.

Bible Activities and Application

1. Read Titus 2:4-5. Explain how this verse could he thought of as a job description for what we as mothers are to teach and what we as daughters are to learn.

2. Make a list of the seven things the younger women are to learn. Then brainstorm ways in which you can begin preparations for fulfilling that list.

3. Resolve to do one or two of these activities if you don't already have them as responsibilities.

    ❧ Make a menu plan and shopping list.

    ❧ Do the shopping and prepare a meal.

    ❧ Take over the ironing chores for a week.

    ❧ Organize a chore chart and manage younger siblings in their work,

Journal Topics

1. What are your feelings towards becoming a wife and mother? Is it something you anticipate with eagerness or caution?

2. Write a prayer for a child you may have in the future.

What is there in the vale of life
Half so delightful as a wife;
When friendship, love, and peace combine
To stamp the marriage bond divine?
William Cooper (1731-1800)

Men are what their mothers made them.
Ralph Waldo Emerson (1803-1882)

Journal Response

_____
_____
_____
_____
_____
_____
_____
_____
_____
_____
_____
_____
_____
_____
_____
_____
_____
_____
_____
_____
_____
_____
_____
_____
_____
_____
_____
_____
_____
_____
_____
_____
_____
_____

❧ 29 ❧

Choosing a Life Work

"She wants to make a success, not only in her work, but in her life, so that as much good as possible will be the result of her having lived."

Discussion Questions

1. Why is it good for a girl to know a way of earning a living even if she never uses it?

2. Why is a girl of today at an advantage over her grandmother in choice of life's work? What is a disadvantage?

3. What are three considerations to make when choosing a career?

4. Why are nursing and teaching "noble" professions?

5. What must be avoided if a girl goes out to work?

Bible Activities and Application

1. Read the following verses and jot down what role
   God plays in your life's work.

   - Esther 4:14

   - Ecclesiastes 2:24

   - Isaiah 45:1-5

   - Luke 1:15-17

   - Galatians 1:15-16

2. Read these verses and note what God says in regard
   to your attitude toward work.

   - Ecclesiastes 5:19

   - Matthew 13:22-23

   - John 6:27

   - Titus 2:11-15

3. Start today to pray that God will show you clearly
   what He wants you to do as your life's work.

Journal Topics

1. Describe the life's work you are considering and explain your choice.

2. Tell about a person who you think is a success.

Blessed is he who has found his work;
Let him ask no other blessedness.
Thomas Carlyle (1795-1881)

They will be none the less sweet for a little
wisdom, and the golden hair will not curl less
gracefully outside the head by reason of there
being brains within.
Thomas Henry Huxley (1825-1895)

Journal Response

❧ 30 ❧

A Consecrated Life

"That is why I wish to talk to you about the consecrated life, the life all given in humble, willing service to God."

Discussion Questions

1. What is the definition of success as God intended?

2. What is the consecrated life?

3. Explain the analogy of consecration of earthly vessels under Mosaic law and the consecration of the heart today.

4. What are some of the special kinds of work that are particularly the Lord's? Have you considered if God has a special call on your life? If so, what is it? What are the two ways in which you can prepare?

5. Using the analogy of a potter, describe how God might mold his clay. Why would it take longer for some than others?

Bible Activities and Application

1. Read Isaiah 29:16 and Romans 9:20-21. Who is the potter? Who is the clay? What is the main idea in relation to how God is molding you? What purpose does He have for you?

2. Look up the word consecration. What does it mean in view of this chapter?

3. Read 2 Timothy 2.20-22. These verses talk about consecrating yourself to God. Go through the passage verse by verse, rewriting them in your own words. Personalize verse 21 by inserting your name.

Journal Topics

1. Explain how the first quote relates to living a consecrated life.

2. Think ahead to where you will be in ten to fifteen years. How do you picture yourself living in humble service to God?

How far that little candle throws his beams!
So shines a good deed in a weary world.
William Shakespeare (1564-1616)

The greater part of happiness or misery
depends on our dispositions, not our
circumstances.
Martha Washington (1731-1802)

Journal Response

২ 31 ৎ

A Pure Heart

"The heart can be made a fit temple into which the Lord can be invited to be the inhabitant."

Discussion Questions

1. Describe something you have seen that represents purity and untouched beauty.

2. Why do you think purity and cleanliness in nature or anything else are admired and appreciated?

3. How does the natural sinfulness of the heart affect striving for a pure heart? What are some common feelings that may interfere with a pure heart? How can this be overcome?

4. Do you think it is possible to live a completely pure life with a heart that is a fit temple for the Lord to inhabit?

5. What does a person who has given her heart to God experience?

Bible Activities and Application

1. Read Romans 12:2a. How do we transform our minds?

2. Read Psalm 119:2, 9, 11, 37. For each verse, write down the action the writer took and what request or statement he made.

3. Read Psalm 119:9. What does this verse tell you about how a young man or woman can keep his or her way pure?

Journal Topics

1. Find a way to incorporate the following suggestions into your quiet time in order to keep your thoughts pure. Use your journal to begin the process.

   ❧ READ—Read one chapter at a time, not isolated verses.

   ❧ STUDY—Seek what God is saying to you and record your findings.

   ❧ MEMORIZE—Hide God's word in your heart to fight all your temptations.

   ❧ MEDITATE—Mull over God's word and its meaning. It will give you insight and keep your heart pure.

Such are your habitual thoughts, such also will be the character of your mind, for the soul is dyed by the thoughts.
Marcus Aurelius (121-180 A.D.)

Despite everything, I believe that people are really good at heart.
Anne Frank (1929-1945)

Journal Response

❧ 32 ❧

A Few Faults Discussed

"There are many faults, but every one of them can be overcome if a girl sets her heart to be victorious."

Discussion Questions

1. What do you think the author means by "seasons of inward searching"? Have you experienced this?

2. Name and describe the seven faults presented in this chapter.

3. Explain strategies for battling each fault.

4. With which of these do you struggle? Relate some situations that have arisen because of these faults.

5. How can we have hope in spite of our faults and attempt to deal with them?

Bible Activities and Application

1. Match each verse to the issue it discusses:

   ꙮ Proverbs 18:11

   ꙮ 2 Corinthians 13:5

   ꙮ 1 Timothy 6:6

   ꙮ James 1:6

   indecisiveness
   self-examination
   contentment
   selfishness

2. Are you exhibiting any of these problems? Do you desire to be content? Ask the Lord to show you if any of these areas are in need of improvement.

3. Memorize I John 1:9.

Journal Topics

1. Explain why the first quote is often quite true.

2. Write honestly about the faults you have struggled with and your efforts to overcome them.

The greatest of faults, I should say, is to be conscious of none.
Thomas Carlyle (1795-1881)

And often times excusing of a fault
Doth make the fault worse by the excuse.
William Shakespeare (1564-1616)

Journal Response

_____

_____

_____

_____

_____

_____

_____

_____

_____

_____

_____

_____

_____

_____

_____

_____

_____

_____

_____

_____

_____

_____

_____

_____

_____

_____

_____

_____

_____

_____

_____

_____

Afterword

The two editions of **Beautiful Girlhood** differ after Chapter 32. Chapter 34 of Mabel Hale's original version appears in the revised edition as Chapter 33 and Hale's original Chapter 33 was eliminated completely.

We feel that both of these chapters serve as a summary of what **Beautiful Girlhood** tries to achieve. Hale wanted girls to understand the wonderful experiences that await them as they become women: physically, spiritually, and emotionally.

Although at times Hale's words may seem quaint and a bit old-fashioned, they remain true. In spite of changes in society, a girl can still aspire to set a code of conduct for herself and, with guidance, can follow it. Hale wrote, "There are no fluctuations in the standards that will always govern what is right and clean and proper in true, upright, Christian manhood and womanhood."

I sincerely hope that no matter which version of **Beautiful Girlhood** you and your daughter used with this guide that it was a pleasant and memorable journey for both of you. The path to womanhood is never an easy one, but perhaps you found it less difficult with the opportunity to read, think, and discuss the wisdom contained in the words of Mabel Hale.

Shelley

The Three Weavers
Plus Companion Guide

A Father's Guide to Guarding His Daughter's Purity

Annie Fellows Johnston,
Revised and Expanded by Robert and Shelley Noonan

Father's play a crucial role in their daughter's lives. Studies show that close healthy father/daughter relationships create a sense of competence in a daughter's academic ability and a strong sense of femininity in girls. In addition, they are less likely to engage in early sexual behavior.

Fathers understandably feel awkward discussion purity with their daughter. The Three Weaver Plus Companion Guide is intended to be a comfortable tool for fathers to mentor their daughter through a charming allegory, discussion guide, Bible study, and activities.

"In the current world of compromise, Robert and Shelley Noonan have superbly crafted a must-read book for every caring father desiring to his daughter the best wedding gift of all—a pure heart!"

Chuck Black- husband, father and author of The Kingdom Series

The Three Weavers Plus Companion Guide.............................$13.95
(Group Discounts Available)

Related Materials

Principles of the Three Weavers ~ Six Keys to Guarding Your Daughter's Heart (CD or MP3)

The first man a little girl falls in love with is her father. Yet fathers are often unaware of the crucial role they play in their daughter's lives as they grow from little girls to young women. How do you begin to capture your daughter's heart and discover together? How do you encourage her to stay pure? How can you ensure she marries a godly man? Join Shelley Noonan as she presents six keys to guarding your daughter's heart!

So Much More Than Sugar and Spice (CD or MP3)

What are little girls made of? Sugar and Spice and everything nice. While this is not the only information a father has about his daughter, dads are often unaware of who their daughter is and what makes her tick. In this session, dads will discover what kind of father he is, what his parenting style is, and how his parenting style affects his little girl. Based on The Three Weavers.

B'twistandB'tweenBlog.com

Join our newly created blog community designed for Moms taking their daughter on the journey through *Beautiful Girlhood* and *The Companion Guide to Beautiful Girlhood!* As I spoke with women using our product they all had one thing in common. They desperately desired encouragement and even companionship as they escort their daughter on this passage into womanhood.

B'twixt and B'tween Blog was created to fill that heart's cry. Mothers are invited to partake of a little TLC and community as they sign up for the RSS feed when classes begin each fall. Each week, a new post will be available to coincide with the chapter you are doing with your daughter. Or, you can independently visit the site and gain uplifting advice and ideas when you peruse the archived chapter posts.

Each post is divided into lessons that will coincide with the chapter. Each lesson includes a note of encouragement, the character focus of the week called the B'Attitude, Memory Verse, Activities, Ponder and Post, and Suggested Resources. All of these features are designed to enrich the road trip through Beautiful Girlhood.

Come join us on the journey at **Btwixtandbtweenblog.com!**

Beyond Beautiful Girlhood Plus Companion Guide

Margaret Elizabeth Sangster,
Revised and Expanded by Shelley Noonan

"Each young woman has a peculiar and individual question to settle. What she is now forecasts what she may be and indeed what she will be, twenty years hence."
Margaret E. Sangster

What are you doing to make sure your daughter is prepared for life? Do you long to instruct and prepare your daughter as she approaches the years of her womanhood? Are you looking for a way to reveal to her what the Lord has done in your life?

Introducing the next step in the Beautiful Girlhood series! At last, a Mother and Daughter bible study for young women in the daybreak of their lives! This study is perfect for girls ages 13-18 and their mothers to enjoy together! Written originally in 1900, this classic volume has been updated to include journal questions, Bible study, togetherness activities, resource sections and much more! This format makes this book an ideal tool for mothers to mold their daughter and teach them how to manage their home, life, and spirit.

Beyond Beautiful Girlhood Plus Companion Guide (240 pages).........$16.95 (Group Discounts Available!)

Related Materials

Beyond Beautiful Girlhood Organizational Charts CD
Do you ever wish you had helpful charts to help you organize your home life and spirit? Search no longer! Here are seven reproducible charts found in Beyond Beautiful Girlhood Plus Companion Guide. Designed to help you manage your home, life, and spirit!

Beyond Beautiful Girlhood (CD or MP3)
All Mama's know their daughter's transition from beautiful girlhood to beyond beautiful girlhood can be the most frightening and exciting of times. Discover how to prepare your daughter in three key areas of her life. Shelley will give you encouraging examples and practical application to equip you to prepare your daughter for the day when she will manage her home, her life, and her spirit!

www.PumpkinSeedPress.net

Wholesale Information

All three of our books adapt well to group studies!

If you are interested in special pricing
for churches, organizations, girls clubs, and co-ops,
please contact us here for a discount schedule.

Pumpkin Seed Press
43668 355th Ave
Humphrey, Ne 68642
www.pumpkinseedpress.net
info@pumpkinseedpress.net
402-923-1682